Good things take time

Copyright © 2019 by Writeables
All rights reserved. This book or any portion thereof
may not be reproduced or used in any manner whatsoever
without the express written permission of the publisher.
Printed in the United States of America
First Printing, 2019

Grateful Thoughts

THIS WEEK I AM GRATEFUL FOR

I AM BLESSED TO HAVE THESE PEOPLE IN MY LIFE

5 REASONS TO BE THANKFUL

1
2
3
4
5

MOOD METER

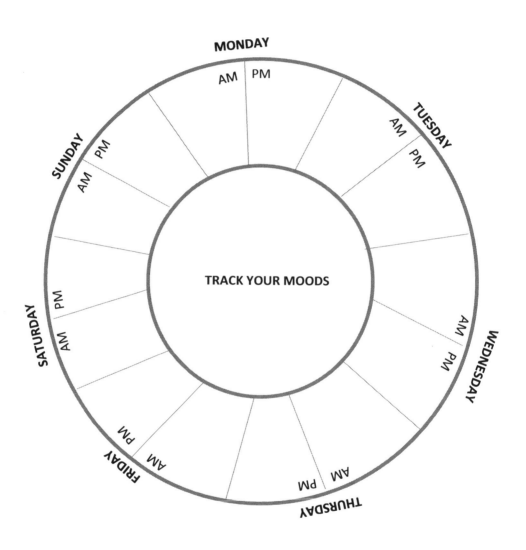

COLOR SCALE

Me Time

Write down the things that make you happy. Then, check the box every day that you spend some time doing that activity.

Do what makes you Happy

Affirmations

DAILY AFFIRMATIONS

IDEAS & PROMPTS

I'm in charge of how I feel today, and I'm choosing to be happy.

I'm brave enough to climb any mountain.

I have the power to change my story.

I've decided that I'm good enough.

No one can make me feel inferior.

My strength is greater than my struggle.

I'll use my failures as a stepping stone.

It's not their job to like me. It's mine.

Success will be my driving force.

The only person who can defeat me, is me.

I dare to be different.

I do not need other people to be happy.

I deserve love, happiness and success.

I am loved and I am wanted.

I will not apologize for being myself.

My Mood Today

DRAWING THAT DESCRIBES YOUR **FEELINGS**

It's just a bad day, Not a bad life

Notes:

Positive Thinking

SELF CARE TO DO LIST:

- [ ]
- [ ]
- [ ]
- [ ]
- [ ]
- [ ]
- [ ]
- [ ]
- [ ]
- [ ]
- [ ]
- [ ]
- [ ]
- [ ]

PHYSICAL NEEDS

EMOTIONAL NEEDS

HOW I FEEL TODAY

I WANT TO WORK ON...

Self Care Checklist

GOALS	M	T	W	T	F	S	S
Got enough rest	○	○	○	○	○	○	○
Spent time outdoors	○	○	○	○	○	○	○
Drank enough water	○	○	○	○	○	○	○
Spent time doing Something that makes me happy.	○	○	○	○	○	○	○
Went for a walk or exercised.	○	○	○	○	○	○	○
Spent time with family	○	○	○	○	○	○	○
Meditated	○	○	○	○	○	○	○
Connected with friends	○	○	○	○	○	○	○
_____	○	○	○	○	○	○	○
_____	○	○	○	○	○	○	○
_____	○	○	○	○	○	○	○

Self Care Log

HOW I CAN **MINIMIZE THE NEGATIVITY** IN MY LIFE

POSITIVE STEPS I CAN TAKE TO BE HAPPY

Self Reflection

SELF REFFLECTION: WHAT MAKES YOU HAPPY?

Each failure brings you one step closer to success

AFFIRMATION:

Personal Goals

MY SELF GOALS FOR THIS YEAR:

2 THINGS I CAN CHANGE TO MEET MY GOALS:

MY GREATEST OBSTACLE GOING FORWARD:

Good things take time

Notes:

Self Care

DAILY INSPIRATION

WATER INTAKE:

FITNESS GOALS

One day at a time...

THANKFUL FOR

DAILY MEALS

BREAKFAST:

LUNCH:

DINNER:

SNACKS:

Mental Health Monitor

DAILY

WEEKLY

PERSONAL REFLECTIONS

Mood Murals

CREATE A SKETCH THAT REPRESENTS YOUR **MOOD**

REFLECTIONS:

Self Care Goals

TIME FRAME	MY GOALS	STEPS I'LL TAKE

be wild ~ be true ~ be happy

Positive Thinking

POSITIVE THOUGHTS:
WRITE DOWN YOUR FAVORITE INSPIRATIONAL PHRASE

Do what makes you Happy

AFFIRMATION:

Notes:

Self Care Techniques

MIND   **BODY**

MOOD METER

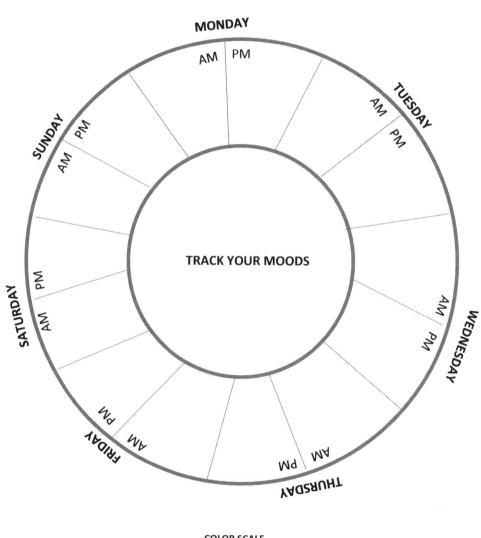

COLOR SCALE

Grateful Thoughts

THIS WEEK I AM GRATEFUL FOR

I AM BLESSED TO HAVE THESE PEOPLE IN MY LIFE

5 REASONS TO BE THANKFUL

1
2
3
4
5

Me Time

Write down the things that make you happy. Then, check the box every day that you spend some time doing that activity.

Activity	S	M	T	W	T	F	S
	☐	☐	☐	☐	☐	☐	☐
	☐	☐	☐	☐	☐	☐	☐
	☐	☐	☐	☐	☐	☐	☐
	☐	☐	☐	☐	☐	☐	☐
	☐	☐	☐	☐	☐	☐	☐
	☐	☐	☐	☐	☐	☐	☐
	☐	☐	☐	☐	☐	☐	☐
	☐	☐	☐	☐	☐	☐	☐

☆ *Do what makes you Happy* ☆

Affirmations

DAILY AFFIRMATIONS

IDEAS & PROMPTS

I'm in charge of how I feel today, and I'm choosing to be happy.

I'm brave enough to climb any mountain.

I have the power to change my story.

I've decided that I'm good enough.

No one can make me feel inferior.

My strength is greater than my struggle.

I'll use my failures as a stepping stone.

It's not their job to like me. It's mine.

Success will be my driving force.

The only person who can defeat me, is me.

I dare to be different.

I do not need other people to be happy.

I deserve love, happiness and success.

I am loved and I am wanted.

I will not apologize for being myself.

Notes:

My Mood Today

DRAWING THAT DESCRIBES YOUR **FEELINGS**

It's just a bad day, Not a bad life

Positive Thinking

SELF CARE TO DO LIST:

- [ ]
- [ ]
- [ ]
- [ ]
- [ ]
- [ ]
- [ ]
- [ ]
- [ ]
- [ ]
- [ ]
- [ ]
- [ ]
- [ ]
- [ ]

PHYSICAL NEEDS

EMOTIONAL NEEDS

HOW I FEEL TODAY

I WANT TO WORK ON...

Self Care Checklist

GOALS	M	T	W	T	F	S	S
Got enough rest	○	○	○	○	○	○	○
Spent time outdoors	○	○	○	○	○	○	○
Drank enough water	○	○	○	○	○	○	○
Spent time doing Something that makes me happy.	○	○	○	○	○	○	○
Went for a walk or exercised.	○	○	○	○	○	○	○
Spent time with family	○	○	○	○	○	○	○
Meditated	○	○	○	○	○	○	○
Connected with friends	○	○	○	○	○	○	○
_____	○	○	○	○	○	○	○
_____	○	○	○	○	○	○	○
_____	○	○	○	○	○	○	○

Self Care Log

HOW I CAN MINIMIZE THE NEGATIVITY IN MY LIFE

POSITIVE STEPS I CAN TAKE TO BE HAPPY

Self Reflection

SELF REFFLECTION: WHAT MAKES YOU HAPPY?

Each failure brings you one step closer to success

AFFIRMATION:

Notes:

Personal Goals

MY SELF GOALS FOR THIS YEAR:

2 THINGS I CAN CHANGE TO MEET MY GOALS:

MY GREATEST OBSTACLE GOING FORWARD:

Good things take time

Self Care

DAILY **INSPIRATION**

DAILY **MEALS**

BREAKFAST:

LUNCH:

DINNER:

SNACKS:

WATER INTAKE:

FITNESS **GOALS**

One day at a time...

THANKFUL **FOR**

Mental Health Monitor

DAILY

WEEKLY

PERSONAL REFLECTIONS

Mood Murals

CREATE A SKETCH THAT REPRESENTS YOUR **MOOD**

You become what you believe

REFLECTIONS:

Self Care Goals

TIME FRAME	MY GOALS	STEPS I'LL TAKE

be wild ~ be true ~ be happy

Notes:

Positive Thinking

POSITIVE THOUGHTS:
WRITE DOWN YOUR FAVORITE INSPIRATIONAL PHRASE

Do what makes you Happy

AFFIRMATION:

Self Care Techniques

MIND   **BODY**

MOOD METER

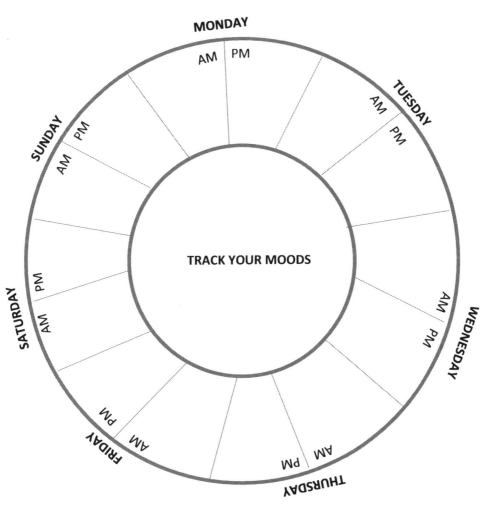

COLOR SCALE

Grateful Thoughts

THIS WEEK I AM GRATEFUL FOR

I AM BLESSED TO HAVE THESE PEOPLE IN MY LIFE

5 REASONS TO BE THANKFUL

1
2
3
4
5

Me Time

Write down the things that make you happy. Then, check the box every day that you spend some time doing that activity.

	☐☐☐☐☐☐☐
	☐☐☐☐☐☐☐
	☐☐☐☐☐☐☐
	☐☐☐☐☐☐☐
	☐☐☐☐☐☐☐
	☐☐☐☐☐☐☐
	☐☐☐☐☐☐☐
	☐☐☐☐☐☐☐

☆ *Do what makes you Happy* ☆

Notes:

Affirmations

DAILY AFFIRMATIONS

IDEAS & PROMPTS

I'm in charge of how I feel today, and I'm choosing to be happy.

I'm brave enough to climb any mountain.

I have the power to change my story.

I've decided that I'm good enough.

No one can make me feel inferior.

My strength is greater than my struggle.

I'll use my failures as a stepping stone.

It's not their job to like me. It's mine.

Success will be my driving force.

The only person who can defeat me, is me.

I dare to be different.

I do not need other people to be happy.

I deserve love, happiness and success.

I am loved and I am wanted.

I will not apologize for being myself.

My Mood Today

DRAWING THAT DESCRIBES YOUR **FEELINGS**

It's just a bad day, Not a bad life

Positive Thinking

SELF CARE TO DO LIST:

- [ ] _____
- [ ] _____
- [ ] _____
- [ ] _____
- [ ] _____
- [ ] _____
- [ ] _____
- [ ] _____
- [ ] _____
- [ ] _____
- [ ] _____
- [ ] _____
- [ ] _____
- [ ] _____

PHYSICAL NEEDS

EMOTIONAL NEEDS

HOW I FEEL TODAY

I WANT TO WORK ON...

Self Care Checklist

GOALS	M	T	W	T	F	S	S
Got enough rest	○	○	○	○	○	○	○
Spent time outdoors	○	○	○	○	○	○	○
Drank enough water	○	○	○	○	○	○	○
Spent time doing Something that makes me happy.	○	○	○	○	○	○	○
Went for a walk or exercised.	○	○	○	○	○	○	○
Spent time with family	○	○	○	○	○	○	○
Meditated	○	○	○	○	○	○	○
Connected with friends	○	○	○	○	○	○	○
_____	○	○	○	○	○	○	○
_____	○	○	○	○	○	○	○
_____	○	○	○	○	○	○	○

Self Care Log

HOW I CAN MINIMIZE THE NEGATIVITY IN MY LIFE

POSITIVE STEPS I CAN TAKE TO BE HAPPY

Notes:

Self Reflection

SELF REFFLECTION: WHAT MAKES YOU HAPPY?

Each failure brings you one step closer to success

AFFIRMATION:

Personal Goals

MY SELF GOALS FOR THIS YEAR:

2 THINGS I CAN CHANGE TO MEET MY GOALS:

MY GREATEST OBSTACLE GOING FORWARD:

Good things take time

Self Care

DAILY INSPIRATION

DAILY MEALS

BREAKFAST:

LUNCH:

DINNER:

SNACKS:

WATER INTAKE:

FITNESS GOALS

One day at a time...

THANKFUL FOR

Mental Health Monitor

DAILY	WEEKLY

PERSONAL REFLECTIONS

Mood Murals

CREATE A SKETCH THAT REPRESENTS YOUR **MOOD**

You become what you believe

REFLECTIONS:

Notes:

Self Care Goals

TIME FRAME	MY GOALS	STEPS I'LL TAKE

be wild ~ be true ~ be happy

Positive Thinking

POSITIVE THOUGHTS:
WRITE DOWN YOUR FAVORITE INSPIRATIONAL PHRASE

Do what makes you Happy

AFFIRMATION:

Self Care Techniques

MIND **BODY**

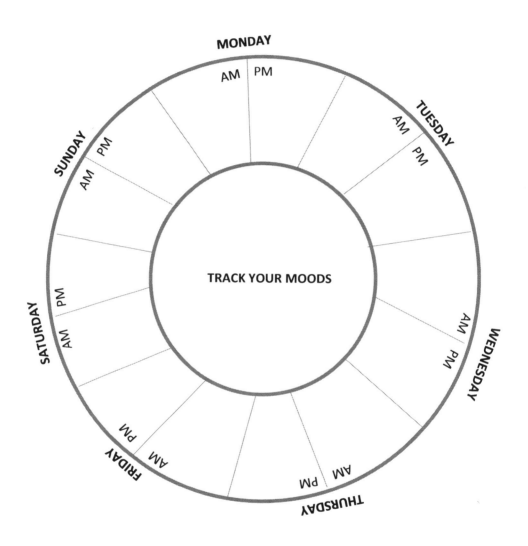

Grateful Thoughts

THIS WEEK I AM GRATEFUL FOR

I AM BLESSED TO HAVE THESE PEOPLE IN MY LIFE

5 REASONS TO BE THANKFUL

1
2
3
4
5

Notes:

Me Time

Write down the things that make you happy. Then, check the box every day that you spend some time doing that activity.

	☐☐☐☐☐☐☐
	☐☐☐☐☐☐☐
	☐☐☐☐☐☐☐
	☐☐☐☐☐☐☐
	☐☐☐☐☐☐☐
	☐☐☐☐☐☐☐
	☐☐☐☐☐☐☐
	☐☐☐☐☐☐☐

☆ **Do what makes you Happy** ☆

Affirmations

DAILY AFFIRMATIONS

IDEAS & PROMPTS

I'm in charge of how I feel today, and I'm choosing to be happy.

I'm brave enough to climb any mountain.

I have the power to change my story.

I've decided that I'm good enough.

No one can make me feel inferior.

My strength is greater than my struggle.

I'll use my failures as a stepping stone.

It's not their job to like me. It's mine.

Success will be my driving force.

The only person who can defeat me, is me.

I dare to be different.

I do not need other people to be happy.

I deserve love, happiness and success.

I am loved and I am wanted.

I will not apologize for being myself.

My Mood Today

DRAWING THAT DESCRIBES YOUR FEELINGS

It's just a bad day, Not a bad life

Positive Thinking

SELF CARE TO DO LIST:

- [ ]
- [ ]
- [ ]
- [ ]
- [ ]
- [ ]
- [ ]
- [ ]
- [ ]
- [ ]
- [ ]
- [ ]
- [ ]
- [ ]

PHYSICAL NEEDS

EMOTIONAL NEEDS

HOW I FEEL TODAY

I WANT TO WORK ON...

Self Care Checklist

GOALS	M	T	W	T	F	S	S
Got enough rest	○	○	○	○	○	○	○
Spent time outdoors	○	○	○	○	○	○	○
Drank enough water	○	○	○	○	○	○	○
Spent time doing Something that makes me happy.	○	○	○	○	○	○	○
Went for a walk or exercised.	○	○	○	○	○	○	○
Spent time with family	○	○	○	○	○	○	○
Meditated	○	○	○	○	○	○	○
Connected with friends	○	○	○	○	○	○	○
_____	○	○	○	○	○	○	○
_____	○	○	○	○	○	○	○
_____	○	○	○	○	○	○	○

Notes:

Self Care Log

HOW I CAN **MINIMIZE THE NEGATIVITY** IN MY LIFE

POSITIVE STEPS I CAN TAKE TO BE HAPPY

Self Reflection

SELF REFFLECTION: WHAT MAKES YOU HAPPY?

Each failure brings you one step closer to success

AFFIRMATION:

Personal Goals

MY SELF GOALS FOR THIS YEAR:

2 THINGS I CAN CHANGE TO MEET MY GOALS:

MY GREATEST OBSTACLE GOING FORWARD:

Good things take time

Self Care

DAILY **INSPIRATION**

DAILY **MEALS**

BREAKFAST:

WATER INTAKE:

LUNCH:

FITNESS **GOALS**

DINNER:

One day at a time…

SNACKS:

THANKFUL **FOR**

Mental Health Monitor

DAILY

WEEKLY

PERSONAL REFLECTIONS

Notes:

Mood Murals

CREATE A SKETCH THAT REPRESENTS YOUR **MOOD**

You become what you believe

REFLECTIONS:

Self Care Goals

TIME FRAME	MY GOALS	STEPS I'LL TAKE

be wild ~ be true ~ be happy

Positive Thinking

POSITIVE THOUGHTS:
WRITE DOWN YOUR FAVORITE INSPIRATIONAL PHRASE

Do what makes you Happy

AFFIRMATION:

Self Care Techniques

MIND

_____
_____
_____
_____
_____
_____
_____
_____
_____
_____
_____
_____

BODY

_____
_____
_____
_____
_____
_____
_____
_____
_____
_____
_____
_____

MOOD METER

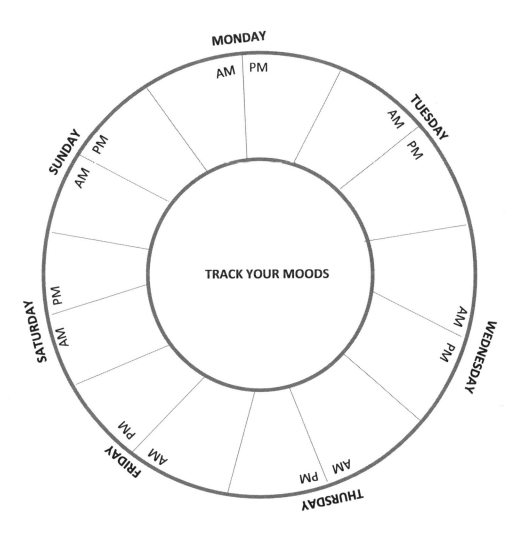

COLOR SCALE

Notes:

Grateful Thoughts

THIS WEEK I AM GRATEFUL FOR

I AM BLESSED TO HAVE THESE PEOPLE IN MY LIFE

5 REASONS TO BE THANKFUL

1.
2.
3.
4.
5.

Me Time

Write down the things that make you happy. Then, check the box every day that you spend some time doing that activity.

	☐☐☐☐☐☐☐
	☐☐☐☐☐☐☐
	☐☐☐☐☐☐☐
	☐☐☐☐☐☐☐
	☐☐☐☐☐☐☐
	☐☐☐☐☐☐☐
	☐☐☐☐☐☐☐
	☐☐☐☐☐☐☐

Do what makes you Happy

Affirmations

DAILY AFFIRMATIONS

IDEAS & PROMPTS

I'm in charge of how I feel today, and I'm choosing to be happy.

I'm brave enough to climb any mountain.

I have the power to change my story.

I've decided that I'm good enough.

No one can make me feel inferior.

My strength is greater than my struggle.

I'll use my failures as a stepping stone.

It's not their job to like me. It's mine.

Success will be my driving force.

The only person who can defeat me, is me.

I dare to be different.

I do not need other people to be happy.

I deserve love, happiness and success.

I am loved and I am wanted.

I will not apologize for being myself.

My Mood Today

DRAWING THAT DESCRIBES YOUR **FEELINGS**

It's just a bad day, Not a bad life

Positive Thinking

SELF CARE TO DO LIST:

- [ ]
- [ ]
- [ ]
- [ ]
- [ ]
- [ ]
- [ ]
- [ ]
- [ ]
- [ ]
- [ ]
- [ ]
- [ ]
- [ ]

PHYSICAL NEEDS

EMOTIONAL NEEDS

HOW I FEEL TODAY

I WANT TO WORK ON…

Notes:

Self Care Checklist

GOALS	M	T	W	T	F	S	S
Got enough rest	○	○	○	○	○	○	○
Spent time outdoors	○	○	○	○	○	○	○
Drank enough water	○	○	○	○	○	○	○
Spent time doing Something that makes me happy.	○	○	○	○	○	○	○
Went for a walk or exercised.	○	○	○	○	○	○	○
Spent time with family	○	○	○	○	○	○	○
Meditated	○	○	○	○	○	○	○
Connected with friends	○	○	○	○	○	○	○
_____	○	○	○	○	○	○	○
_____	○	○	○	○	○	○	○
_____	○	○	○	○	○	○	○

Self Care Log

HOW I CAN **MINIMIZE THE NEGATIVITY** IN MY LIFE

POSITIVE STEPS I CAN TAKE TO BE HAPPY

Self Reflection

SELF REFFLECTION: WHAT MAKES YOU HAPPY?

Each failure brings you one step closer to success

AFFIRMATION:

Personal Goals

MY SELF GOALS FOR THIS YEAR:

2 THINGS I CAN CHANGE TO MEET MY GOALS:

MY GREATEST OBSTACLE GOING FORWARD:

Good things take time

Self Care

DAILY INSPIRATION

WATER INTAKE:

FITNESS GOALS

One day at a time...

THANKFUL FOR

DAILY MEALS

BREAKFAST:

LUNCH:

DINNER:

SNACKS:

Notes:

Mental Health Monitor

DAILY

WEEKLY

PERSONAL REFLECTIONS

Mood Murals

CREATE A SKETCH THAT REPRESENTS YOUR **MOOD**

You become what you believe

REFLECTIONS:

Self Care Goals

TIME FRAME	MY GOALS	STEPS I'LL TAKE

be wild ~ be true ~ be happy

Positive Thinking

POSITIVE THOUGHTS:
WRITE DOWN YOUR FAVORITE INSPIRATIONAL PHRASE

Do what makes you Happy

AFFIRMATION:

Self Care Techniques

MIND   **BODY**

_____   _____
_____   _____
_____   _____
_____   _____
_____   _____
_____   _____
_____   _____
_____   _____
_____   _____
_____   _____
_____   _____
_____   _____

Notes:

ONE DAY AT A TIME

1	2	3	4
5	6	7	8
9	10	11	12
13	14	15	16
17	18	19	20
21	22	23	24
25	26	27	28
29	30	31	

ONE DAY AT A TIME

1	2	3	4
5	6	7	8
9	10	11	12
13	14	15	16
17	18	19	20
21	22	23	24
25	26	27	28
29	30	31	

ONE DAY AT A TIME

1	2	3	4	
5	6	7	8	
9	10	11	12	
13	14	15	16	
17	18	19	20	
21	22	23	24	
25	26	27	28	
29	30	31		

ONE DAY AT A TIME

1	2	3	4
5	6	7	8
9	10	11	12
13	14	15	16
17	18	19	20
21	22	23	24
25	26	27	28
29	30	31	

ONE DAY AT A TIME

1	2	3	4
5	6	7	8
9	10	11	12
13	14	15	16
17	18	19	20
21	22	23	24
25	26	27	28
29	30	31	

ONE DAY AT A TIME

1	2	3	4
5	6	7	8
9	10	11	12
13	14	15	16
17	18	19	20
21	22	23	24
25	26	27	28
29	30	31	

ONE DAY AT A TIME

	1	2	3	4
	5	6	7	8
	9	10	11	12
	13	14	15	16
	17	18	19	20
	21	22	23	24
	25	26	27	28
	29	30	31	

ONE DAY AT A TIME

1	2	3	4
5	6	7	8
9	10	11	12
13	14	15	16
17	18	19	20
21	22	23	24
25	26	27	28
29	30	31	

ONE DAY AT A TIME

	1	2	3	4
	5	6	7	8
	9	10	11	12
	13	14	15	16
	17	18	19	20
	21	22	23	24
	25	26	27	28
	29	30	31	

ONE DAY AT A TIME

1	2	3	4
5	6	7	8
9	10	11	12
13	14	15	16
17	18	19	20
21	22	23	24
25	26	27	28
29	30	31	

ONE DAY AT A TIME

1	2	3	4
5	6	7	8
9	10	11	12
13	14	15	16
17	18	19	20
21	22	23	24
25	26	27	28
29	30	31	

ONE DAY AT A TIME

1	2	3	4
5	6	7	8
9	10	11	12
13	14	15	16
17	18	19	20
21	22	23	24
25	26	27	28
29	30	31	

Made in the USA
San Bernardino, CA
13 June 2019